AUTISM Love

The You Got This

with Doses of Love & Encouragement Along the Way

Cause Some Days We Need a Hug

(or a nap, or a shower, or to know that everything might just work out)

Journal for Caregivers

KI PRODUCTIONS
Where every story matters

ISBN: 978-1-961605-20-6

This Journal Belongs to:

_____

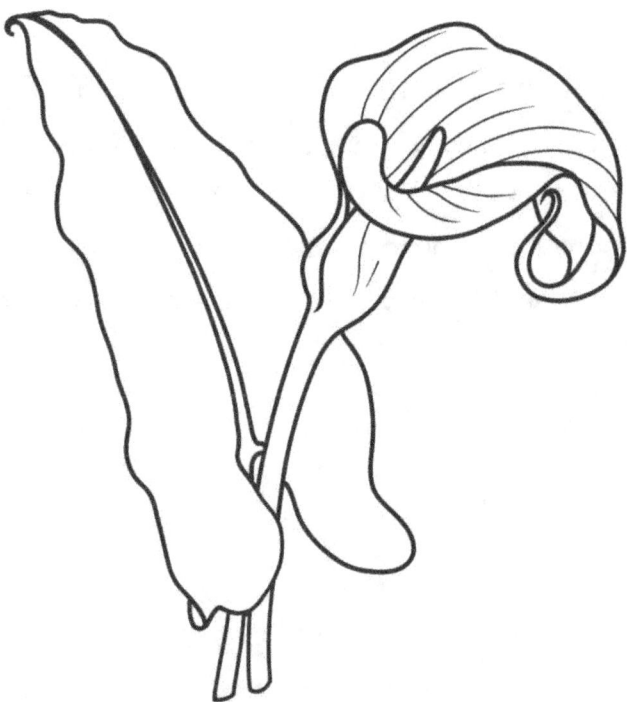

Dear Caregiver,

First, thank you for all you do. As a mom of two sons with exceptional needs, I have walked through lonely, hard days with nothing more to give. I've questioned my abilities to endure, felt ill-equipped as a mother, and times my own mental health required attention. I designed this journal based on what I needed most during my most difficult moments. My hope is that the pages in this journal will comfort & encourage you precisely when you need it.

May you be supported when you feel alone, encouraged when you need to be lifted, nudged to rest and care for yourself when you need it, and inspire you to imagine the future and know your work is not in vain.

Know that this is YOUR journal — there is no right or wrong way to proceed: start in the back, jump around, write when you feel like it, color when you're not in the mood to write, respond to quotes or prompts, or don't. Write everyday or once a week. Just make time for you — because you matter too!

Love & Prayers,
Marya

Feeling Alone

The Needs We Share

to be welcome

to be invited

to be heard

to be believed

to be understood

to be seen

to be valued

Let's Start Here...
You Are Not Alone.

It's lonely but when you meet someone
who gets it. it's transforming.
~ Melody Statham Cameron

Date:

Date:

_____

_____

_____

_____

_____

_____

_____

_____

_____

_____

_____

_____

_____

_____

_____

_____

Date:

_____

_____

_____

_____

_____

_____

_____

_____

_____

Knowing how to be solitary is central to the art of loving. When we can be alone, we can be with others without using them as a means of escape.

~ bell hooks

Date:

_____

_____

_____

_____

_____

_____

_____

_____

_____

Date:

_____

_____

_____

_____

_____

_____

_____

_____

_____

_____

_____

_____

_____

_____

_____

_____

_____

Date:

_____

_____

_____

_____

_____

_____

_____

_____

_____

_____

_____

So now, all alone or not, you gotta walk
ahead. Thing to remember is if we're all
alone, then we're all together in that too.
~ Cecelia Ahern

Date:

_____

_____

_____

_____

_____

_____

_____

_____

_____

Date: _____

_____

_____

_____

_____

_____

_____

_____

_____

_____

_____

_____

_____

_____

_____

_____

_____

_____

_____

Date:

_____

_____

_____

_____

_____

_____

_____

_____

_____

_____

At the innermost core of all loneliness is a deep and powerful yearning for union with one's lost self.

~ Brendan Behan

Date:

Date:

_____

_____

_____

_____

_____

_____

_____

_____

_____

_____

_____

_____

_____

_____

_____

_____

_____

Date:

God has placed you where you're at in this
very moment for a reason. Remember that
and trust He is working everything out.
~ unknown

Date:

_____

_____

_____

_____

_____

_____

_____

_____

Date:

_____

_____

_____

_____

_____

_____

_____

_____

_____

_____

Laughter, song, and dance create emotional
and spiritual connection; they remind us of
the one thing that truly matters when we
are searching for comfort, celebration,
inspiration, or healing: We are not alone.

~ Brené Brown

Date:

I am a part of all that I have met.

~ Lord Tennyson

We need to remember to teach our children that solitude can be a much-to-be-desired condition. Not only is it acceptable to be alone, at times it is positively to be wished for. In silence, we listen to ourselves, and in the quietude, we may even hear the voice of God.

~ Maya Angelou

_____

_____

_____

_____

_____

_____

_____

_____

_____

Date:

Date:

_____

_____

_____

_____

_____

_____

_____

_____

_____

_____

I don't think the worst thing that could happen to me is raising a child with special needs. I think the worst thing is to raise a child who is cruel to those with special needs.

~ unknown

Date:

_____

_____

_____

_____

_____

_____

_____

_____

_____

Date:

Date:

_____

_____

_____

_____

_____

_____

_____

_____

_____

_____

_____

We can all fight against loneliness by
engaging in random acts of kindness.
~ Gail Honeyman

Date:

_____

_____

_____

_____

_____

_____

_____

_____

_____

Date:

Date:

_____

_____

_____

_____

_____

_____

_____

_____

_____

_____

Take one day at a time. Today, after all, is the tomorrow you worried about yesterday.
~ Billy Graham

Date:

Date:

Date:

_____

_____

_____

_____

_____

_____

_____

_____

_____

_____

Realize that you are not alone, that we are
in this together, and most importantly
that there is hope.
~ Deepika Padukone

Date:

Date:

Date:

_____

_____

_____

_____

_____

_____

_____

_____

_____

_____

Possible Journal Prompts

♥ What are your top 3 needs at this moment?

♥ How do you receive encouragement?

♥ How do you talk to yourself? Do you use affirmations?

♥ Write a list of all the things that make you smile.

♥ Write a list or entry of gratitude – who & what you're grateful for.

♥ What are your top 3 needs at this moment?

♥ What is something that you control & needs to change?

I had so much yet to learn about myself
and the world. My son taught me more
than I will likely ever teach him.
And I am grateful.
~ Marya Patrice Sherron

Storms make oaks take roots.

~ proverb

Date: _____

_____

_____

_____

_____

_____

_____

_____

_____

_____

Date:

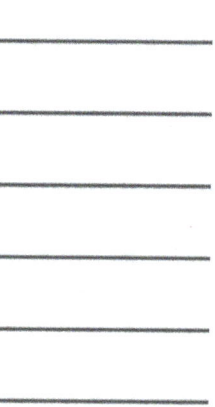

Date:

_____

_____

_____

_____

_____

_____

_____

_____

_____

_____

Fitting in allows you to blend in with everyone else, but being different allows you to be yourself, to be unique and to be more creative.

~ Sonya Parker

Date:

Date:

You have a choice each and every single day. I choose to feel blessed. I choose to feel grateful. I choose to be thankful. I choose to be happy.

~ Unknown

Date: _____

_____

_____

_____

_____

_____

_____

_____

_____

_____

Date:

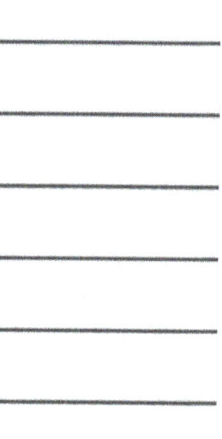

Date:

_____

_____

_____

_____

_____

_____

_____

_____

_____

_____

Parents of children with special needs create
their own world of happiness and believe in
things that others cannot yet see.

~ unknown

Date:

Date:

Date:

_____

_____

_____

_____

_____

_____

_____

_____

_____

_____

Parenthood is about raising and celebrating the child you have, not the child you thought you'd have. It's about understanding your child is exactly the person they are supposed to be. And, if you're lucky, they might be the teacher who turns you into the person you're supposed to be.
~The Water Giver

_____

_____

_____

_____

_____

_____

_____

_____

_____

Date:

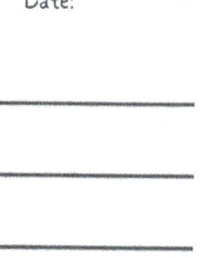

Date:

_____

_____

_____

_____

_____

_____

_____

_____

_____

_____

_____

Life is slippery. Here, take my hand.

~ H. Jackson Brown, Jr.

Some of the most wonderful people
are the ones who don't fit into boxes.

~ unknown

Always
Unique
Totally
Intelligent
Sometimes
Mysterious

While we try to teach our children all
about life, our children teach us what life
is all about.
~ Angela Schwindt

Date:

_____

_____

_____

_____

_____

_____

_____

_____

_____

Date:

The disability is not the problem. The accessibility is the problem.
~ Mohamed Jemni

Date:

_____

_____

_____

_____

_____

_____

_____

_____

_____

Date:

You are now in a secret world. You'll see things you never imagined: ignorance, rudeness, and discrimination.

But you'll also witness so many everyday miracles, and you'll know it. You won't think a milestone is just a milestone, you'll know it's a miracle.

You'll treasure things most people wouldn't think twice about.

You'll become an advocate, an educator, a specialist, and a therapist, but most of all, you'll be a parent to the most wonderful child.

~ Geraldine Renton

Date:

_____

_____

_____

_____

_____

_____

_____

_____

_____

_____

Until you have a kid with special needs, you
have no idea of the depth of your strength,
tenacity and resourcefulness.

~ unknown

Date:

Date:

Date:

_____

_____

_____

_____

_____

_____

_____

_____

_____

_____

Embrace the unique way your child is blooming – even if it's not in the garden you imagined.

Date:

_____

_____

_____

_____

_____

_____

_____

_____

_____

Date:

The world would be a paradise of
peace and justice if global citizens
shared a common definition of love
which would guide our thoughts
and action.

~ bell hooks

Date:

_____

_____

_____

_____

_____

_____

_____

_____

_____

_____

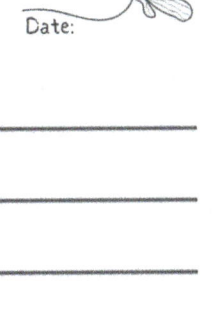

Date:

_____

_____

_____

_____

_____

_____

_____

_____

_____

_____

_____

Date:

Date:

_____

_____

_____

_____

_____

_____

_____

_____

_____

_____

Self-Care

Rest and self-care are so important. When you take time to replenish your spirit, it allows you to serve from the overflow. You cannot serve from an empty vessel.
~ Eleanor Brown

Dahlias

Possible Journal Prompts

💗 What are your top 3 needs at this moment?

💗 Write about your self-care practices?

💗 Words are powerful – write a list of affirmations.

💚 Write about your Love Language (time, gifts, acts of kindness, or words of affirmation).

🧡 We can never express too much gratitude — write about all you're currently thankful for.

💗 Write about you daily water in-take, exercise and overall diet.

💙 What is something that you have been putting off, but would be SO good for you to do?

Self-care is the number one solution to helping somebody else. If you are being good to yourself and your body and your psyche, that serves other people better, because you will grow strong enough to lift someone else up.

~ Mary Lambert

_____

_____

_____

_____

_____

_____

_____

_____

_____

_____

Be KiND
to yourself

Date:

_____
_____
_____
_____
_____
_____
_____
_____
_____
_____
_____
_____
_____
_____
_____
_____
_____

Self
love

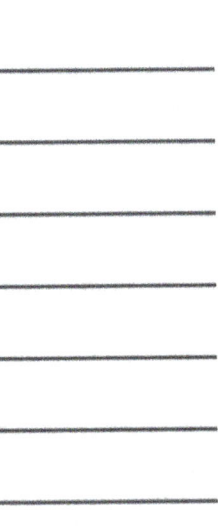

Date:

_____

_____

_____

_____

_____

_____

_____

_____

_____

_____

YOU aRe
eNOUGH

You are in a much better position to serve others when your basic needs are met and your 'tank is full'.

~ Michael Hyatt

Date:

_____

_____

_____

_____

_____

_____

_____

_____

_____

_____

GIVE
yourself
a BREAK

Date:

_____

_____

_____

_____

_____

_____

_____

_____

_____

_____

_____

_____

_____

_____

_____

_____

_____

PROTECT
YOUR
PEACE

Date:

_____

_____

_____

_____

_____

_____

_____

_____

_____

_____

breathe deeply

Promise me you'll always remember...
you're braver than you believe, stronger
than you seem, smarter than you think,
and loved more than you know.
~ Christopher Robin

Date:

_____

_____

_____

_____

_____

_____

_____

_____

_____

Date:

_____

_____

_____

_____

_____

_____

_____

_____

_____

_____

_____

_____

_____

_____

_____

_____

BE PATIENT
WITH
YOURSELF

Every survival kit should include a sense of humor.

~ Unknown

Date:

Date:

_____

_____

_____

_____

_____

_____

_____

_____

_____

_____

_____

_____

_____

_____

_____

_____

_____

_____

_____

Self-care
IS EMPOWERMENT

Date:

_____

_____

_____

_____

_____

_____

_____

_____

_____

_____

Sometimes the difficult things that happen in our lives put us directly on the path to the best things that will ever happen to us.

~ unknown

Date:

_____

_____

_____

_____

_____

_____

_____

_____

_____

_____

Date:

Care

Date:

_____

_____

_____

_____

_____

_____

_____

_____

_____

_____

Self-care is a deliberate choice to gift
yourself with people, places, things,
events, and opportunities that
recharge our personal battery and
promote whole health — body, mind,
and spirit.
~ Laurie Buchanan, Ph.D.

A Flower

for

You

It's okay to take time for yourself. We give so much of ourselves to others, and we need to be fueled both physically and mentally. If we are in balance, it helps us in all our interactions.

~ Faith Hill

Date:

Date:

be
you

Date:

_____

_____

_____

_____

_____

_____

_____

_____

_____

_____

The time to relax is when you don't have
time for it.
~ Sydney J. Harris

Date:

_____

_____

_____

_____

_____

_____

_____

_____

_____

Date:

_____

_____

_____

_____

_____

_____

_____

_____

_____

_____

_____

_____

_____

_____

_____

_____

_____

SHINE

Date:

_____

_____

_____

_____

_____

_____

_____

_____

_____

_____

_____

glow

Do something today that your future self
will thank you for.

~ unknown

Date:

Date:

_____

_____

_____

_____

_____

_____

_____

_____

_____

_____

_____

_____

_____

_____

_____

_____

_____

_____

**eNJoY
ToDay**

Date:

_____

_____

_____

_____

_____

_____

_____

_____

_____

_____

Magic

In dealing with those who are undergoing great suffering, if you feel 'burnout' setting in, if you feel demoralized and exhausted, it is best, for the sake of everyone, to withdraw and restore yourself. The point is to have a long-term perspective.

~ The Dalai Lama

_____

_____

_____

_____

_____

_____

_____

_____

_____

_____

Soul

Date:

Love

Date:

_____

_____

_____

_____

_____

_____

_____

_____

_____

_____

_____

_____

I have come to believe that caring for myself is not self-indulgent. Caring for myself is an act of survival.

~ Audre Lorde

Date:

_____

_____

_____

_____

_____

_____

_____

_____

_____

Date:

Yeah

Date:

_____

_____

_____

_____

_____

_____

_____

_____

_____

_____

Self-care is giving the world
the best of you. instead of
what's left of you.
                ~ Katie Reed

Imagine

Poppies

When you read a book, you acquire knowledge.
When you look at a flower, your imagination grows wild.
~ Michael Bassey Johnson, Night of a Thousand Thoughts

Possible Journal Prompts

♥ What are your top 3 needs at this moment?

♥ Talk about your dreams – are there dreams abandoned, forgotten, but still burn deep within you?

♥ What is your idea of a perfect day?

♥ Write about an adventure or challenge you would like to conquer?

♥ Who is the most inspiring person you know?

♥ Write a letter of encouragement to yourself.

♥ Imagine yourself one year from now — how are you different?

Knowledge of what is possible is the
beginning of happiness.
~ George Santayana

Date:

Date:

_____

_____

_____

_____

_____

_____

_____

_____

_____

_____

_____

_____

_____

_____

_____

_____

_____

Date:

_____

_____

_____

_____

_____

_____

_____

_____

_____

_____

Each day of our lives we make deposits in
the memory banks of our children.
~ Charles R. Swindoll

Date:

Date:

_____

_____

_____

_____

_____

_____

_____

_____

_____

_____

_____

_____

_____

_____

_____

_____

_____

_____

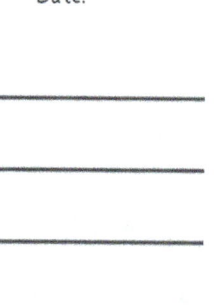
Date:

_____

_____

_____

_____

_____

_____

_____

_____

_____

_____

It is not our differences that divide us. It is our inability to recognize, accept and celebrate those differences.

~ Audre Lorde

Date:

_____

_____

_____

_____

_____

_____

_____

_____

_____

Date:

Date:

_____

_____

_____

_____

_____

_____

_____

_____

_____

_____

A diagnosis can't predict the extraordinary love you will have for your child.

~ Tara McCallan

Date:

_____

_____

_____

_____

_____

_____

_____

_____

_____

Date:

Date:

_____

_____

_____

_____

_____

_____

_____

_____

_____

_____

To be nobody but yourself in a world doing its best to make you everybody else means to fight the hardest battle any human can ever fight and never stop fighting.

~ E.E. Cummings

Date:

Date:

_____

_____

_____

_____

_____

_____

_____

_____

_____

_____

_____

_____

_____

_____

_____

_____

Date:

_____

_____

_____

_____

_____

_____

_____

_____

_____

_____

Wherever you are, at any moment, try and find something beautiful. A face, a line out of a poem, the clouds out of a window, some graffiti, a wind farm. Beauty cleans the mind.

~ Matt Haig, Reasons to Stay Alive

You

Are

Loved

Hang on tight and get ready for the wildest, saddest, happiest, most challenging and most rewarding ride of your life!

~ Sylvia Phillips

Date:

_____

_____

_____

_____

_____

_____

_____

_____

_____

_____

Date:

_____

_____

_____

_____

_____

_____

_____

_____

_____

_____

C'est toujours l'imagination qui l'emporte
sur la volonté, sans aucune exception.

It is always the imagination that wins over
the will, without exception.
~ Émile Coué

Date:

Date:

Date:

_____

_____

_____

_____

_____

_____

_____

_____

_____

_____

_____

The power of
imagination is
strongest
in the place of
solitude.

~ Sunday Adelaja

Most people see what is and never see
what can be.

~ Albert Einstein

Date:

_____

_____

_____

_____

_____

_____

_____

_____

_____

_____

Date:

Date:

Love

in

every

shade

Everything that is new or uncommon raises a pleasure in the imagination, because it fills the soul with an agreeable surprise, gratifies its curiosity, and gives it an idea of which it was not before possessed.

~ Joseph Addison

Date:

Date:

Date:

_____

_____

_____

_____

_____

_____

_____

_____

_____

_____

_____

Developing our imagination, the language of
the soul, allows Spirit to work through us
as we answer our calling.
~ Linda Naiman

Date:

Date:

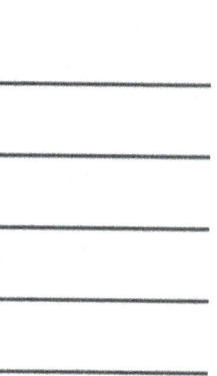

Date:

_____

_____

_____

_____

_____

_____

_____

_____

_____

_____

Daydreams are fertile ground for the imagination to soar. As you sit absorbed in a problem, notice when you get lost in a day dream. What were you just thinking of? Your unconscious is a rich source of images, ideas and experiences that lead to new connections, and fresh thinking.

~ Linda Naiman

Never Forget...
You Are Equipped
You Are Chosen
You Are Enough
...You Are Loved
~ Marya Patrice Sherron

AUTISM
Love

The You Got This

with Doses of Love & Encouragement Along the Way

Cause Some Days We Need a Hug

(or a nap, or a shower, or to know that everything might just work out)

Journal for Caregivers

www.ingramcontent.com/pod-product-compliance
Lightning Source LLC
Chambersburg PA
CBHW051006140626
46546CB00016B/881